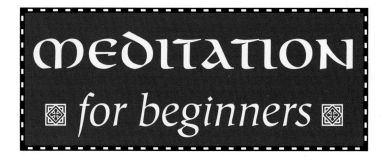

MEDITATION
for beginners

NAOMI OZANIEC

Headway · Hodder & Stoughton

ACKNOWLEDGEMENTS

The publishers would like to thank the following for giving permission to reproduce copyright photographic material in this book:

Bruce Coleman Ltd, cover; The Bridgeman Art Library, pp 6 and 7; Camera Press (UK) Ltd, p 12; Japan National Tourist Organisation, p 13; Ngakpa Chogym, *Rainbow of Liberated Energy*, Shaftesbury, Element Books Ltd, 1986, p 14; Biblioteque Nationale, pp 15 and 16; Tharpa Publications Ltd, London, p 20; Philip Emmett, Lincoln, p 21; Daniel A Keintz, p 23; Mel Thompson, p 26; Dharmachari Aloka, *Friends of the Western Buddhist Order*, Norwich, Surlingham, p 27; John Dugger and David Medella, p 32; Mary Evans Picture Library, pp 35 and 40; Philip Rawson, *Tantra: The Indian Cult of Ecstasy*, Thames & Hudson, p 41; Ajit Mookerjee, *Kundalini*, Thames & Hudson, pp 42 and 43; by courtesy of the Victoria & Albert Museum, p 44; Durham University Oriental Museum, bottom p 47; Tharpa Publications Ltd, London, p 52; Panos Pictures, p 55; Douglas Dickins Photo Library, p 57; The Bridgeman Art Library, p 60; NASA, p 62; William Bloom, *Meditation In A Changing World*, Gothic Image, 1986, p 65; Werner Forman Archive, p 73; Ann and Bury Peerless, pp 76 and 79.
Every effort has been made to trace and acknowledge ownership of copyright. The publishers will be glad to make suitable arrangements with any copyright holders whom it has not been possible to contact.

Cataloguing in Publication Data is available from the British Library

ISBN 0 340 64835 X

First published 1993 as *Meditation in a Week*
Re-published 1995 as *Meditation for Beginners*

© Naomi Ozaniec 1993, 1995

Typeset by Rowland Phototypesetting Limited, Bury St Edmunds, Suffolk.
Printed in Hong Kong for Hodder & Stoughton Educational, a division of Hodder Headline Plc, 338 Euston Road, London NW1 3BH by Colorcraft Ltd.

CONTENTS

This book is a practical guide to meditation practice. Meditation is to be found throughout the great religions of the world although you do not need to have a religious belief to take it up.

Every religion has both an exoteric and esoteric aspect. The exoteric aspect enshrines dogma, belief and creed. The esoteric aspect enshrines spiritual practice, exercises and techniques, particularly meditation. One path emphasises belief, the other stresses experience. It is not uncommon to develop spiritual philosophy as the practice of meditation awakens you.

The clear instructions in this book will allow you to begin to meditate from the start. Seven themes are introduced, each theme containing several exercises. You may return to all of the exercises at a later date. These exercises are based on traditional meditations from both East and West and are essentially simple to perform but difficult to master. Meditation is a mental discipline but it is also a way of life. When you work through the book try to meditate at the same time each day. This will help you to establish a personal routine. You should aim to sit in meditation for about fifteen minutes each day. It is always a good idea to use the same subject over and over again.

Do not expect to achieve mental mastery immediately, you are just beginning. It is said that a journey of a thousand miles begins with a single step. This book might just be that first step. So let's begin by looking at the basic things that we need to know as we set out on that journey.

WHY MEDITATE?

We each bring our own reasons for taking up meditation. These can be many and varied, but they usually fall into several main categories – health, stress prevention, self-realisation and spiritual impulse.

It is not uncommon for doctors to recommend meditation. Meditative techniques, particularly those involving creative visualisation, are now commonly taught to patients with cancer. There is a very strong link between the mind and the body. Disease often follows anxiety, stress or depression. Meditation proceeds from a state of physical relaxation and uses the mind to calm the body. Deep relaxation creates certain conditions within the body which are physically beneficial. The lactate concentration of the blood, which is closely linked to anxiety levels, decreases sharply. The breathing pattern which is consciously established in meditation creates conditions of serenity and calm. Many physical changes can be measured during meditation. Even the brain rhythms alter during meditation, different brain patterns reflecting the various types of meditation. Meditation can also help us to cope with everyday stress. As we cope more effectively with stress, we are more able to contribute to our own good health.

Meditation is an holistic discipline. It creates change at all levels of being including the physical, emotional and mental. It also has the power to awaken us to the spiritual levels of our being, not through handed down dogma but through experience. Meditation enables us to discover who we really are and what we may achieve. It brings us to a state of self-realisation which is the highest expression of the human nature.

The principles of meditation

Meditation is a mental discipline. It is a state of mind in which all thoughts are concentrated upon a single point, namely the subject of the exercise. It takes patience and persistence to develop the power of concentration. The mind will naturally wander to other things. The attention must be returned to the subject over and over again. It can be very frustrating to discover just how easily the attention wanders. The subject of the meditation is rather like a target. Stray thoughts will prevent us from hitting the bull's eye. When we are able to hold the concentration steady we can begin to reap the benefits. This sustained state of concentration leads to personal realisation. A realisation may be an insight, a new idea, a flash of intuition or simply a good feeling. In time these personal realisations snowball and bring about lasting changes for the individual. In Zen the experience of non duality, a profound realisation, is called **satori**. Our first realisations will not be of this magnitude, but nevertheless we are experiencing something of the same resonance, a dynamic breakthrough in consciousness.

Preparation for meditation

You will need to take a few moments to prepare the surroundings in which you are going to meditate. The key is very simple – be comfortable, you will be sitting still for a while. You might need to loosen any tight clothing. Excessively hot or cold rooms will simply distract you. Do not sit in a dark room, this will encourage drowsiness. Do not sit in the glare of a bright light, this will strain the eyes. A slightly dimmed light or gentle daylight will provide suitable lighting conditions. Some people light a candle to signify the start of the practice. This is acceptable, but never become dependent upon external stimuli. You carry the conditions for meditation within.

Posture is important to all meditation practice. Choose a firm chair which enables you to sit upright. Place your feet firmly on the ground. This keeps you in touch with the earth. Do not meditate lying down or sitting in an armchair as you will soon be asleep. Keep the spine straight. Sit in an alert but poised way. The hands may be folded loosely in the lap or placed one upon each thigh. You do not have to sit cross legged to meditate. The lotus position is fine for experts in Yoga and those brought up to sit like this but it is unattainable for most Westerners, and quite unnecessary.

Become aware of your breathing and allow yourself to breathe more slowly and deeply than you might normally. Mentally follow your breath in and out for a few moments. The deep quiet breathing pattern also helps to bring a sense of calm to the mind and body.

Our pattern of breathing directly reflects our emotional state. When we are upset or angry our breathing becomes chaotic and erratic. By contrast when we are calm, our breathing pattern is regular and rhythmic. In meditation we seek to find a quiet mind, so we begin by establishing a breathing pattern normally associated with quietness and calm. There are also complex breathing patterns for advanced meditative techniques which are designed to bring about specific mental and emotional states.

As we become more aware of our own natural breathing pattern we may discover that we normally breathe using only the top of the lungs. This represents a symbolic defence mechanism. Shallow breathing is related to a shallow contact with life experience. When we deepen the breath we deepen our contact with life. The following breathing pattern, the fourfold breath, is a simple way of establishing a deeper breath from the diaphragm.

The fourfold breath

Breathe in with a deep but comfortable breath from the diaphragm to the count of four.
Hold the breath at the top of the lungs for the count of two.
Breath out slowly to the count of four.
Hold the lungs empty to the count of two.
Start again.

Relaxation technique

Having seated yourself in a suitable chair, establish an appropriate breathing pattern. You are now ready to enter into a state of meditation by following the Relaxation Technique outlined below. This does not mean either physical or mental sloppiness, but a state of relaxed alertness. When you are experienced you will be able to move straight into a state of concentration. The relaxation exercise itself helps develop concentration by using the power of the mind to establish a physical condition.

Relaxation should be done slowly. The mind is simply focused on the different body parts in turn in the following way: turn your attention inwards and mentally repeat the phrase to yourself. After each phrase you should also experience a release of tension in the body itself. Take your time with this exercise.

'The top of my head is relaxing, I feel relaxed.
My face feels relaxed, I am relaxed.
My shoulders and chest feel relaxed, I am relaxing.
My arms and hands feel relaxed, I am relaxing.
My legs and feet feel relaxed, I am relaxing.
I am relaxed. My mind is calm. My body is calm.
I am relaxed. My mind is alert. My mind is awake.'

Jain diagram of the cosmos used for meditation from Rajastan, late 18th century.

Do not rush this stage. When you are experienced this preliminary practice can be dispensed with. It simply helps to take your mind away from the hurly-burly of your everyday activities. Meditation is invariably practised in quiet monastic settings free from the wear and tear of traffic noise and disturbances. You have to make a conscious effort to put yourself far beyond the difficulties of your daily life before you reach the meditation state itself. When you are ready call the subject of your meditation to mind.

Subjects for meditation

The possible subjects for meditation are endless. Each spiritual tradition tends to favour particular subjects. One form of Buddhism uses the body and its natural activities as subjects. Everyday activities such as walking, breathing, moving and resting are brought to the forefront of the mind so that they can be performed mindfully rather than unconsciously. Another branch of Buddhism favours complicated mental images and circular symbolic designs. Both branches of Buddhism focus upon many qualities of being such as loving-kindness, compassion, happiness or joy as subjects for reflective thought. Christian meditations traditionally focus on scenes from the life of Christ or aspects of Christian belief. The Eastern Orthodox church uses icons as subjects for devotional meditations. All traditions draw upon their own special symbols and teachings for meditation subjects. Mantras are a special form of sounded meditation (see Thursday's chapter for more information).

You will have the opportunity to try several approaches as you read this book. When you have gained some experience you may feel confident enough to choose your own subjects and there are many possible subjects around you all the time – living plants, trees, flowing waters. A fifth century Buddhist text lists the four elements earth, air, fire, and water; the colours red, blue, yellow and white; and the notions of space and light as suitable subjects for the student to start with.

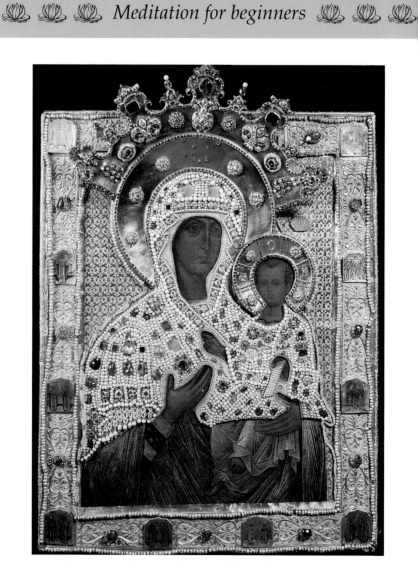

Icons form part of a devotional tradition. The painters prepared themselves with meditations and prayer. Devotees gazed upon the icon as a meditation. Icon of the Virgin, Smolenskaja, Moscow, 16th century, Kremlin Museums, Moscow.

Byzantine Icon of St Gregory, Pushkin Museum, Moscow.

Discovery in meditation

Meditation can be thought of as a journey of discovery into yourself. The realisations that you have are yours alone and these will tell you a great deal about yourself. It is a good idea to keep a meditation diary so that you can record your thoughts and insights. The notes should be written up immediately after the session while the ideas are fresh in your mind. The following example might be helpful.

Date 20th August 1995
Time 8.00–8.20pm
Meditation subject Loving – kindness
Realisations Thought about the qualities of love and kindness, tried to combine them mentally – remembered being shown kindness as a child – kindness seems to be a very innocent quality, it asks nothing back. Imagined what the world would be like without this quality – ghastly thought. Thought of the people I have shown kindness to recently – too few of them – must try to be less self-centred and more sensitive to others.
Difficulties Concentration was patchy. Images of childhood so strong that my mind began to wander off into general reverie. Had to work hard to return my thoughts to the subject.

This personal record will prove invaluable over a period of time. It is exciting to wonder what you may discover about yourself. Now before you begin the exercises get pen and paper and explore your own reasons for being interested in meditation in the first place. Make a list of all the things that you hope meditation might help you to find. This initial list will help to establish a starting point for you. In the future you can look back on it to see how far your experience measured up to your expectations. You may also discover that your expectations themselves changed through your experience. In any event your first thoughts about meditation are of personal value, so record them.

Many people take up meditation in order to combat stress. Others come to meditation through ill health. Many doctors now teach meditative techniques as part of an holistic approach. Still others seek introspection, a way of knowing themselves better. Some people are simply curious about meditation. Others used meditation to deepen an existing spiritual alignment. All these reasons are perfectly valid. You might explore what changes you think meditation might bring to the physical, emotional, mental and spiritual parts of your life. When you have spent time and thought compiling your list you are ready to turn to the first exercise.

HELPLINE

Is there an optimum time for meditation?
The early morning is recommended. You should be refreshed after sleep. It will also prepare you for the day ahead.

I have no religious belief, does this matter?
This does not matter at all. You do have a belief system though you may not have articulated it to yourself. You believe in your own power to create change in your life. This is a good starting point. Meditation will give you the opportunity to explore your own beliefs.

My family is totally against me taking up meditation, they believe it is a weird foreign practice.
Meditation is both a perfectly respectable and a highly respected tradition. It is found in both Christianity and Judaism, which are the two major religions of the Western world. It is not foreign. You will discover that people generally are poorly informed about meditation, but there is nothing whatsoever for anyone to be concerned about.

FINDING YOUR SPACE

'We speak at times of an expanding universe, what we really mean, is an expanding consciousness.'

The Tibetan

Making space

When we begin meditation we usually have to make a space in our lives. Our daily routine seems to be so busy that finding even a fifteen-minute space seems impossible. We may initially have to reschedule something, perhaps get up a bit earlier, go to bed a bit later, or change our priorities. Finding space in our lives is the first task. When we have done this, we have to make space in our minds for the practice of meditation to take place.

Every journey appears to have a starting point, that is the moment when we consciously set out towards a goal. The decision to begin meditation expresses our intention to look more deeply at ourselves and the world in which we live, to penetrate beyond appearance in the search for meaning.

When we think of space we naturally think of interstellar space, vast, silent, mysterious and distant. We think of distance beyond measure, time beyond count, infinity. We do not associate these far horizons with ourselves and the perceived limitations of our lives. Yet the rich symbolism of space has something to teach us as we set out to look behind appearances. The mystery and infinite nature of space is truly awe inspiring and mind stretching. Space symbolises what can be called cosmic consciousness, the conscious awareness of the whole.

In Buddhism the state of Enlightenment is called **Shunyata**, the void. Shunyata, emptiness, is paradoxically full. 'Emptiness is form, form is emptiness.' Space is not empty, even though it appears so from our perspective.

When we first set out on the path of meditation, we must make a space in both our lives and our minds for meditation to take place. As our consciousness expands, limitations drop away and we become aware of spaciousness at all levels of being.

Discovering *your* space, the starting point for the journey is also paradoxical, for space is owned by no-one. Yet when we set out, we establish a claim to something that we identify as being *ours*. This may be our belief system, our aspirations, our intentions, our psychic territory.

By claiming our beliefs and values in consciousness, we are able to examine and understand our own world view. Being conscious of our belief system prepares us for expansion, change and growth, spaciousness.

By contrast our everyday lives appear very crowded, crammed with tasks and responsibilities. We seem to lack personal space, sometimes even physical space. We can find no space in life for ourselves. We feel pressured and stressed. Meditation creates space in the mind, brings conscious pauses between thoughts and gives us a perspective on life. We are enabled to raise ourselves above the demands of everyday life and observe our own actions. This process of detachment creates space in our lives, freeing us from instinctive responses, habitual actions and knee-jerk replies.

Our minds like our lives teem with plans, memories, ideas, words and thoughts. We become so used to this state of being that in time we don't even notice it. The rushing stream of consciousness, thoughts mainly without purpose and idle chatter, is ever present like an internal white noise. Everything is hurried, all mental space is filled. It is only when we take the trouble to observe the process that we can evaluate its effect upon us. A mind that is full is like an untidy cupboard that spills its contents whenever the door is opened. It has no space for insight, creativity or applied thought.

Science and medicine are now paying much more attention to the relationship between mind and body. We know that the state of mind has a direct bearing upon health. A mind without space for repose or rest establishes a blueprint which the body will in time duplicate.

The first step in meditation involves looking into the mind and its busy contents. When we become conscious of space within our minds, we will find that we have made room for thoughts and realisations of a new order to be born. Creativity, insight and intuition can only come into being when there is space for us to be receptive to the still small voice of inspiration.

Awaken yourself to the extraordinary mystery of space. Go out and observe the night sky and meditate on what you see. Become aware of immensities beyond measure. Consciously seeking your space will eventually enable you to find your space as part of the heavens here on earth.

Zazen, shi-ne and exercises in mindfulness are the simplest and the safest practices to perform without special guidance. The newcomer to meditation practice can take up this kind of exercise by following the simplest of instructions. These basic exercises are complete in themselves and also serve as stepping stones to deeper, more intense mental states. They bring us face-to-face with our own being, our patience, boredom, confusion, irritation, perseverance and determination. They place us firmly in the here and now, the only space where meditation may take root.

Meditation, the inner journey.

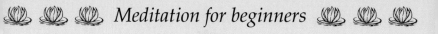

Zazen

Becoming conscious of the contents of the mind is easy in theory and difficult in practice, we simply sit and become aware of what is happening mentally. The basic daily practice in Zen Buddhism is called **zazen**, 'just sitting'. It is described as a practice in which the individual takes aim without having a target. Zazen has no focus other than the mind itself. You can try an exercise of the zazen type whenever you are ready.

Wandering attention will earn a blow across the shoulders from the watchful monk who wields a keisaku.

Exercise 1   Zazen

Simply enter the meditative state by following the steps outlined in the introduction. As you enter the state of meditation, your attention becomes increasingly inwardly focused and decreasingly externally focused. This shift of awareness is often referred to as being centred. When you feel that you are sufficiently inwardly focused, turn your attention deeper and watch your mind at work. It is not the intention to produce thoughts, simply to observe what is happening in the mind. The key is to maintain awareness, to watch the mind working without becoming involved in the mental contents. Try to gain some detachment from the thoughts that fill your mind. Let them pass through like objects on a conveyor belt passing before your eyes. When your session is finished make notes on the thoughts that occupied your mind.

13

You may discover that your mind is filled with a large number of ideas and thoughts in even a short period. Zazen eventually quietens the mind, clearing a space in the crowded thought processes. With space comes a sense of freedom.

Shi-ne

In the Tibetan tradition, this form of practice is called **shi-ne** (she-nay). Like zazen, its essence is to be found in remaining uninvolved in the personal thought process. It is to be practised without expectation. This simple practice brings a sense of being completely here and now, neither caught in the events of the past nor anticipating a future. Ngakapa Chogyam, a Westerner who has unusually achieved recognition as a teacher with the Tibetan tradition, writes that 'this practice of stilling the neurotic thought processes introduces us to a new dimension of ourselves in which there is a sense of spaciousness.'

Tibetan sign for Intrinsic Space.

Mindfulness

Buddhist meditation intentionally develops the sense of the present moment through what is termed 'mindfulness', that is living each moment with full awareness. **Satipatthana**, which is loosely translated as mindfulness, is found in its most detailed and comprehensive form in the Theravada Buddhism of Thailand, Sri Lanka and Burma. The term **sati** implies 'memory' or 'remembrance,' **patthana** stands for **upatthana**, that is 'placing near' or 'keeping present'. Theravada Buddhism claims that it represents the oldest Buddhist lineage, its name means 'Doctrine of the Elders'. In this school mindfulness, or direct awareness, forms a major part of regular practice. The four applications of mindfulness are awareness of the body including the breath, awareness of feelings, awareness of states of mind, and awareness of the contents of the mind.

Mindful meditation throughout the everyday activities of standing, sitting, walking and sleeping.

As a meditative method, mindfulness is both simple yet profound. We can think of it as simply 'paying attention'. Our lives, busy and often stressed, are monuments to oblivion. If we are not aware of ourselves, how can we be aware of life?

In mindfulness practice our attention is focused on the nearest and most inescapable subject, namely ourselves. Mindfulness deliberately brings attention into our lives. Mindfulness slows us down in a frantic world. We hold up a mirror so that we can find ourselves at last.

Mindfulness of the body is directed towards the whole range of physical activities. All physical acts no matter how mundane can be used as the focus for the attentive mind: looking, bending, stretching, drinking, speaking, keeping silent, being awake and falling asleep. Theravada Buddhism has developed the practice of mindfulness to an extraordinary

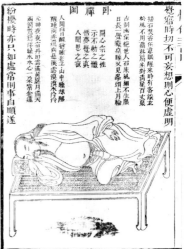

degree. For advanced practitioners even the simple act of placing the foot on the ground has a sixfold division which must be noted separately by the meditator.

Mindfulness of the body is said to bring awareness of movement and of physical location in time and space. The direct attention to minute aspects of posture is intended to break the habitual identification with the body and bring purposeful action. Gradually ordinary life and spiritual practice merge. Mindfulness of the body forces us into the present moment, being fully here and now.

Mindfulness of the body commences with mindfulness of breathing. We can begin to become mindful of the flow of breath by tuning into this pattern during the day. The quiet observation of the natural flow of the breath without regulation or alteration brings calmness of mind and body and serves as a preparation for concentration.

There are many exercises in Buddhism which take the individual through the first steps in attention to more sensitive and refined practices in awareness. Even if we cannot follow these exercises in their most complicated form, we can gain some benefit by applying the principles of mindfulness to our daily lives.

Exercise 2

Ideally the exercise of mindfulness should fill the whole day. This is not practical outside strictly regulated conditions. Being mindful for even an hour will give you the flavour of this approach.

The subject for this meditation will be the body itself. Become fully aware of your bodily posture, paying particular attention to the four basic postures of going, standing, sitting and lying down. These will naturally flow one into the other as you move. Become aware of the posture you have adopted, and of any change that takes place including the intention to change position. Also note any sensation connected with each posture. The aim is simply to note what is happening continuously and simply.

You might like to note how often your attention wandered away from the task in hand, and any feelings that this simple exercise evoked for you. These simple exercises can be quite dull and frustrating. You are imposing a new discipline on the mind, which will often resist.

HELPLINE

I can't get over the feeling that when I sit in zazen I am just wasting my time.

We are so conditioned to be busy all the time that 'just sitting' cuts right across our beliefs. Women especially are conditioned to feel guilty about taking time for themselves. Zazen is an active process, so the time is not wasted. You may well find that zazen proves to be extremely productive, a ten-minute session may bring you increased clarity of thought and calmness of mind which will enable you to deal with the day's tasks more effectively and efficiently.

I keep giving myself reasons for not meditating today. I know these are just excuses.

It is common to experience a great deal of resistance initially to the discipline of meditation. Starting meditation is much like learning to ride an unruly horse. Ask yourself who sets the agenda, you or the 'horse'? Keep your sessions short, don't make the practice onerous and thereby provide reasons for avoiding it.

Meditation in Buddhism

Buddhism evolved from the meditation of Siddharta Gautama who became the Buddha – the fully enlightened one. Meditation is understandably central to all Buddhist practice.

Buddha established the Noble Eightfold Path, the eight principles which bring enlightenment. These are:

Right view
Right resolve
Right speech
Right conduct
Right livelihood
Right effort
Right awareness
Right meditation

There are three major schools of Buddhism and a great many minor ones. The **Hinayana** School is the school of the 'lesser vehicle' which aims to bring enlightenment to those individuals who embrace its teachings. The **Mahayana** School is the school of the 'great vehicle' which aims to bring enlightenment to all sentient beings. Finally the **Varjrayana** School, the 'diamond or indestructible vehicle' presents the most esoteric aspects of Buddhist teachings. Theravada Buddhism belongs to the Hinayana school, and it predominates in Asia. Its texts are predominantly written in Pali. Mahayana Buddhism exists mainly in Tibet and Japan. Its texts are mainly written in Sanskrit.

Zen Buddhism is a unique branch of Mahayana Buddhism which originated with the sixth-century teacher Bodidharma, who summed up the approach of Zen in the following words:

A special tradition outside the scriptures,
No dependence on words,
A direct pointing at man,
Seeing into one's own nature and the attainment of wisdom.

Zen has developed a unique style and approach including an original form of meditation, the **koan**. The koan is like a puzzle without an apparent answer. Its purpose is to 'break asunder the mind of ignorance' and 'open the eye of truth'. Like the little boy in the tale of the Emperor's New Clothes, the Zen mind sees through illusion, cuts through pretence and strikes at reality itself.

Zen assumes that like the walking dead, the classic zombie, we are each in the grip of massed illusions which like a veil stand between us and even the simplest experience. These illusions are even strengthened by intellectual structures and philosophies which straightjacket our responses, expectations and perceptions. Zen has no time for dogma, only for 'direct seeing'. Zen seeks to awaken us to the direct experience of each moment stripped of what we want, like, dislike, expect, project or prefer.

Buddhism is concerned with awakening the Buddha nature, the fully realised state within each person.

1,000-armed Avalokiteshvara. The manifestation of all the Buddha's compassion appearing in the 1,000-armed aspect.

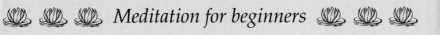
FINDING YOURSELF

'Know thyself.'

Delphic Injunction

This meditator is visibly serene. The body is balanced. The mind is inwardly withdrawn. Harmony exists between mind and body.

21

Who am I?

Our progress continues by thinking about who we are. This is a very important question. It is perhaps the fundamental question of life itself. We all want to know how we have come to be the people we are. It is said that the words 'Know thyself' were written above the doorway of the temple at Delphi. We also find the same idea in the Hindu scriptures. We are not the first people to think about this question.

The philosophical view that we take colours our whole life, our attitude towards others, our aspirations and motivations. We need to think deeply about who we are, not just as individuals in a particular society but as beings in time. Our journey begins with the view that we hold of ourselves today.

When we begin to think about ourselves it is only natural to wonder about the forces that have shaped us. Our upbringing, background, experiences and circumstances have all contributed to our development. We might ask ourselves, are we purely the sum of our total experiences? Do we recognise an individuality which transcends social, biological and economic factors? It is extraordinary to realise the uniqueness of the human being – no two people, even twins, are identical.

We each express an individuality which is quite unique. This uniqueness is an expression of our true self. When we identify with our unique nature, we begin to awaken it within ourselves. We all too frequently identify only with the ego, a small fragment of self, seeking gratification and survival. The ego experience is one of duality and separation. Identity is achieved through staking claims over 'mine' and separating from what is 'not mine'.

Our individuality is often masked by socialisation, unexplored through missed opportunities, stifled even by education. Meditation releases the individuality from shackles and limitations. As we begin to experience the presence of the true self, the individuality, we are enabled to move away from limited expressions of the self, to put aside the mask, to abandon role play and be ourselves. As you set out to find yourself, you will in all probability discover qualities and talents that you never knew existed. Alignment with the true self, becoming the person you were always intended to be, brings a deep sense of fulfilment which extends to all aspects of life. In our everyday life it means that we eventually create the life pattern which best expresses what we have to offer. Unfulfilled people are restless and bored at home and at work, sometimes destructive and usually unhappy. Ego satisfaction is never more than temporary. It is always illusory. The true self is the source of creativity, individual expression and uniqueness.

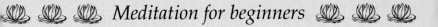

Meditation for beginners

Discovering who you are has often been likened to peeling back the layers of an onion. The image has use, it reminds us that we are indeed composed of many layers. However, in some ways the image is misleading for it suggests that our discoveries bring us the realisation of an ever-diminishing self. In reality it is perhaps more helpful to identify the starting point of the journey as the heart of the 'onion'. As consciousness expands we become aware of successive layers beyond our original conception. As we grasp the reality of each new 'layer' we have to re-evaluate our sense of wholeness. For what was once perceived as complete is in the light of an expanded consciousness perceived to be partial.

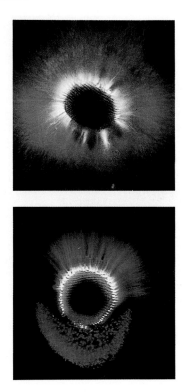

Kirlian photography clearly reveals an energy field surrounding the individual. The quiet mind and the angry mind produce quite different energy patterns. The top Kirlian photograph of a finger shows a state of meditation, the bottom the red of anger. The technique of electrical photography is named after its Russian inventor, Semyon Kirlian.

The expansion of consciousness brings an expansion in all areas of being. We become more conscious of feelings and more able to empathise with others. As we become more conscious of our own thinking, we become increasingly less victimised by idle mental activity. As the self as a whole develops, the impulse towards creativity becomes inescapable. In time we are quite transformed as a new self emerges like a phoenix.

The image that we hold of self is central in our belief system. When we hold a rigid immobile image of self, we invariably hold a closed and restricted view of the greater whole. When we come to an open and expanding view of ourselves we perceive ourselves in a fluid expansive relationship with the greater whole. The philosophical view that we take about the nature of our own being will directly influence actions, behaviour, attitudes and relationships.

We cherish many illusions believing both reality and the 'self' to be stable, constant and based in physicality. This attitude is comforting and reassuring but it is not correct. Matter is built from a sub-atomic base which is in constant movement. We too share a material nature. Yet we are more than simple flesh and blood. The quest for yourself will ultimately reveal this in a way that is meaningful to you personally. Meanwhile take up the search for self with a good heart. You will have many profound and beautiful realisations as you journey.

Exercise 3   Know thyself

The phrase 'know yourself' is an excellent starting point for meditation practice. It can be used as a seed thought, the idea is planted in the mind like a seed which in time will give fruit in the form of personal realisations. Simply sit in a meditative state and dwell upon the meaning and implications of this phrase, which will trigger many ideas, thoughts and perhaps questions for you. Don't forget to record all the thoughts that pass through your mind. You may want to return to these ideas later.

Exercise 4   Recognising

If you are ever to 'know yourself', you will need to spend some time meditating on different aspects of your being. You can begin this quite simply. To help focus your thoughts, find some photographs of yourself at different stages of your life. If you do not have any such photos, you will have to draw on your memories.

Write your name on a piece of paper and lay the photos around it. Have a spare piece of paper handy to make notes. Now sit quietly and look over the photos or cast your mind through your memories. See the many different faces you have presented to the world. Think about what you see and write down anything that comes to mind. What lies before you expresses both unity and diversity, change and constancy. You are in each of the photos, yet you appear quite differently. Simply sit surrounded by these pictures. Write down any thoughts which come to mind.

Exercise 5   Looking

You may use these same photos or memories to gain another level of understanding about yourself. When you are ready return to the photos of yourself.

Sit in a quiet meditative state of mind. Meditate on the many physical appearances and conditions your body has experienced, birth itself, states of sickness and states of health. Think of the many different emotional states you have known: happiness, joy, anger, envy, grief, love, etc. Finally think of all the mental states you have experienced: memory, imagination, dreaming, fantasy and aspiration. Where are you to be found in all these passing experiences?

You will have probably discovered that the mind began to wander a little. It is possible to refine the practice of concentration so that the mind does not wander away from the subject matter. This takes practice and perseverance but it is important if we are to deepen the meditative state. Conclude your session by making notes about your actual span of concentration.

Exercise 6   Breath counting

You can try a simple exercise in pure concentration by using nothing more complicated than your own breathing to focus upon. This is a very old, universal technique for training the mind.

Sit quietly, assume a correct posture for meditation. Become aware of your own breathing. As you complete a breath by breathing in and out, count one. Continue until you have taken ten breaths and counted each one without distraction. If you become distracted or lose your count, go back and start again. You will find that this exercise is far harder to master than it sounds. When you have finished make a few notes about your ability to concentrate on the task in hand. What have you now discovered about your mind?

The Tibetan Wheel of Life

Though we may begin meditation practice by dwelling on ourselves, it is no more than a convenient starting place. We also need to think about our lives in a wider context.

The Tibetan Wheel of Life is an image which enables us to think about ourselves against a background of eternal time. It expresses the central beliefs of Buddhism in visual form. It is painted on the vestibule wall of all Tibetan monasteries.

Tibetan Wheel of Life or Wheel of Becoming.

The two inner circles of the Wheel of Life.

The Wheel of Life, or more correctly the Wheel of Becoming, is divided into four concentric circles. At the hub of the wheel three creatures endlessly chase one another, forever biting each other's tails. The red cockerel represents greed and lust. The green serpent represents anger and hatred. The black pig represents ignorance and delusion.

The second circle is divided equally into two halves each filled with figures. In the black portion those whose volitions have been unhealthy plunge into torment. In the white portion those whose volitions have been healthy and joyous ascend to the realm of the gods.

The next circle is divided into six segments depicting different planes of consciousness. These are, the world of gods, titans, hungry ghosts, the hells, the animal kingdoms and the world of humans.

Finally the last and outer wheel depicts the Conditioned Links of Co-Production, the twelve links which hold us fast to the Wheel of Becoming. These conditions are ignorance, karma-formations, consciousness, name and form, mind and body, the six sense organs, contact, feeling or sensation, craving, coming-to-be, old-age and death. Release from the wheel comes only with personal transcendence.

The wheel itself is clutched by the demon Impermanence. Above the wheel to the right stands the Buddha pointing out the path to Enlightenment. Here is a cosmogram showing the human condition in relation to the universal laws. Ben Shan, a contemporary writer and traveller writes 'in a monastery near the border of Tibet I found a portrait of myself . . . There were all the many aspects of myself painted crude and clear; the pig, the snake, the cock, all animals, angels, demons, titans, gods and men, all heaven and hell, all pleasures and pains, all that went to make me.' He realised that the wheel like a mirror shows us who we are.

Exercise 7   Who am I?

The following meditation begins the quest for self in a structured way. It takes the form of a dialogue. Enter the meditative state. Do not rush through the questions and answers but allow yourself to explore each section before moving on to the next.

Inwardly pose the question, 'Who am I?'
Answer to yourself, 'I am not my body.'
Reflect upon the meaning of this phrase.

Inwardly pose the question, 'Who am I?'
Answer to yourself, 'I am not my emotions.'
Reflect upon the meaning of this phrase.

Inwardly pose the question, 'Who am I?'
Answer to yourself, 'I am not my thoughts.'
Reflect on the meaning of this.

Inwardly pose the question, 'Who am I?'
Answer to yourself, 'I am a centre of pure consciousness.'
Reflect on the meaning of this.

When you have finished record all the thoughts that passed through your mind.

This meditation helps us to break away from limited conceptions of ourselves. When we identify with our bodies we get caught up in physical states of health and sickness. When we identify with our emotions, we identify with moods and become dependent upon others to provide our happiness. When we identify with our thoughts we identify with the contents of the mind, the stream of consciousness. When we identify ourselves with a centre of consciousness, we take a stand which cannot be destroyed by others or circumstances.

This meditation may be practised many times until an inner change of identification really takes place. In life use this meditation when you find yourself identifying too strongly with your body, feelings or thoughts.

You have just begun to meditate. Perhaps you have already made some discoveries about yourself.

Who am I?

HELPLINE

I don't feel worthy as a person. How can I aspire to enlighten others.
Your feelings of being unworthy are quite misplaced. Such feelings are usually a product of education and upbringing. They are part of the negative conditioning which keeps us all prisoners. Instead meditate on your own innate goodness which may have become hidden but is still there.

Meditation in Mahayana Buddhism

Mahayana Buddhism, 'the great vehicle', places its emphasis on helping others, its goal is enlightenment for all sentient beings. A modern teacher, Roshi Philip Kaplaeu, writes 'without enlightening others there is no self enlightenment'. The qualities of cherishing others, compassion and altrusim, are developed through spiritual practice. These qualities which stem from the heart unite people and help to build the human family.

The teaching of the Mahayana school carefully and slowly takes the student along the spiritual path, the Lam Rim, from foundation to enlightenment. The foundation meditation practice in all schools of Buddhism consists in taking refuge in the **Buddha**, the **Dharma** – the teachings – and the **Sangha** – the community of Buddhists. These are The Three Jewels, the Triple Gem. According to Mahayana teachings, 'one takes refuge from now until the essence of enlightenment, Buddhahood, is attained'.

As the student is transformed, becoming increasingly selfless in thought, word and deed, spiritual practice awakens **Bodhicitta**, the mind of enlightenment. The path gradually leads on towards the ideal of the **Bodhisattva**. The Bodhisattva is a fully enlightened being who remains connected to the Wheel of Becoming through a conscious choice in order to bring others to the awakened state. This image is never far away in Mahayana Buddhism.

A chant widely used in Mahayana Buddhism encapsulates the Four Great Vows which express both the path and the goal.

All beings, without number, I vow to liberate.
Endless blind passions, I vow to uproot.
Dharma gates beyond measure, I vow to penetrate.
The Great Way of Buddha, I vow to attain.

FINDING YOUR SYMBOL

'We must learn to see symbols all around us, and then to penetrate behind the symbol to the idea which it should express.'

The Tibetan

Variety and usage of the symbols

A symbol is an image which represents a wide range of meanings other than itself. We are surrounded by symbols in our daily life at the most mundane levels. Companies for example spend considerable time and money devising the logo that will best represent the image they wish to convey. In other words they seek to encapsulate their particular message in symbolic form. Companies, large organisations, even political parties, are willing to change their logos to launch the birth of a new identity. An outdated logo will simply convey an old message. Countries, too, acquire symbols. Britain is still symbolised by the bulldog, Russia by the bear, America by the eagle.

Certain symbols are universal in nature. They are understood, even if not consciously, by peoples across cultural and social divides. These universal symbols often appear in dreams. Jung was amazed to discover that the dreams of modern people could contain symbols which were also the symbols of religions and cultures unknown to them. It was this discovery that lead him to propose the theory of the collective unconscious, a level of mind common to all.

Every religious system has its own special symbols which point to its central teachings. Christianity is, of course, symbolised by the Cross. The seven-branched candlestick, the **menorah** and the six pointed **Star of David** are significant in Judaism. Religious symbols play a central part in ceremonies and rites which might be thought of as symbolism in activity. Symbols also abound in myths and fairy tales. These stories often point towards the mysterious elements of life which can never be fully understood.

A symbol is rich in association and meaning. Even a simple symbolic image may have many levels of meaning. A circle without beginning or end symbolises the endless round of life and the circular pattern of the year. The circle symbolises completion and wholeness. A mandala is a circular pattern symbolically depicting the forces of life. A ring stands for eternal love, unbroken and undying. The circular dance is a sign of community and unbroken tradition. A symbol is like a shorthand or a code representing deep ideas and associations in a simple, brief way.

31

This Tibetan mandala represents a state of exalted consciousness surrounded by subsidiary states. The meditator usually enters the mandala by visualising its imagery in three dimensions. The mandala becomes a mental landscape in which to travel and encounter its regions as internal states of mind.

The sustained exploration of a symbol through meditation can be very fruitful. Understanding can be taken to a deeper level. The mind as a whole is very responsive to symbolic meaning. The human mind naturally produces symbols through the dream process and through free association of ideas. We can learn a great deal about ourselves by working with symbols which arise spontaneously from the deeper levels of the mind. We are now going to look at different approaches to the use of symbols in meditation.

Exercise 8   Spontaneous symbols

We are going to try a very simple passive approach in which we allow images to arise spontaneously.

Have paper and a selection of coloured pens ready. Also keep your record book close at hand. Enter into a meditative state. When you are mentally quiet and inwardly focused, ask yourself, 'Which symbol will represent me as I am today?' Sit quietly and simply allow images to surface and draw whatever comes to mind. You are not seeking great art, simply represent the image for yourself. When it is complete, ask, 'What does this symbol teach me?'

Keep a record of the thoughts that you had during the process. You will be surprised by how much you can discover about yourself and about your chosen symbols. You may even find that you have spontaneously created images which contain universal symbols. Your choice of colours, arrangement, image and details all have something to say. Learning to interpret spontaneous images comes after a wide experience of symbols and their meanings, but today you have made a start.

*The yin-yang symbol for
universal balance and polarity.*

Exercise 9   Symbol incubation

By contrast we can bring a symbol to the mind and actively explore its meaning and association. There are many suitable symbolic images such as the classic yin-yang symbol, the sun, the moon, a circle, a spiral, the elements, earth, air, fire and water, colours, even geometric shapes. Choose your symbol before you start the meditation. You may like to have a picture of your symbol or some other representation of it by your side. Enter a meditative state and bring your selected image clearly to mind. Keep exploring the meanings that you associate with the symbol. When your mind begins to wander, bring it back to the subject of your meditation. There is a great deal to be learned by meditating in this way.

Tibetan set of nine symbolic paintings used for meditation.

Tarot cards present a combination of symbolic images which are best understood through personal meditation.

A symbol and its associated meaning becomes internalised through the process of meditation. Once internalised and absorbed into our psychic structure, the living experience represented by the symbol is available to us through the dynamics of our own being. For instance, meditation using water as a symbol may put us in touch with cleansing forces which may in a real sense enable us to cleanse and renew an aspect of our life. The yin-yang symbol may help us to think about the balance of opposites both in life and in ourselves. Each symbol has something to teach.

Exercise 10   Pathworking

The following meditation combines the ability of the mind to produce a spontaneous image with that of a structured journey. This might be thought of as an active meditation. This form of meditation is common in the Western tradition. You might wish to record the narrative onto a tape before you use it as a meditation. If not, you should memorise the different stages of the mental journey before you start. When you are ready, close your eyes and enter into a meditative state.

Allow yourself to create the following scenes in your imagination. You are walking along a country lane. There are fields to both sides beyond the hedges. To one side you see a stile. You climb over it effortlessly. Now you stand in a field dotted with wild flowers. You hear the sound of insects. Stop for a moment and listen to the sounds. The hedgerow is behind you. Ahead of you the field slopes a little. You see a narrow stream which runs through the field. You make your way towards the stream. You sit by its banks for a while listening to the sound of running water.

The stream is narrow. You decide to cross it, finding your own way of reaching the other side. Now you stand on the far bank. The outer world seems far away. You decide to explore, to look about. How does this field appear to you? Is it grassy or stony, lush or sparse? What kind of flowers, plants or trees grow here? Do you find this place to be open or is your way difficult? You make your way across the field.

At the far side of the field you will find a building which you will see quite clearly. Stand before it. Look carefully at what you see. Find the front door. Go up to the door which will open easily to your touch. Enter the building. You will find a corridor with many doors. All the doors are closed except one which is slightly ajar. Gently push open the door and go into the room beyond. You may see many things here. Pay great attention to all that you see. In the room you will find a table. On the table is a large book bound in leather. You will see that it has your name inscribed on the cover. Stand before the book and compose your thoughts. You have come to look for a sign, a symbol which will teach you something of significance and meaning about yourself. Reflect on what you seek and why. When you are ready, open the book. On the page you will find an image, a picture, a drawing or simply a shape. Look carefully at what you see so that you don't forget.

When you are ready to leave, make your way out of the house. Cross the first field and the stream. Cross the second field and climb back over the stile. Return to normal consciousness and record all the impressions from your journey.

This simple journey will reveal a great deal. Your experience of the field, the stream and the building will each carry symbolic overtones. Try to interpret your impressions for yourself. To understand your symbol better, you can draw it in your note book, meditate upon it or find out more about its historical, cultural or spiritual association. This exercise may be repeated more than once. Different symbols will appear to you at different times as you change.

Symbols are all about us, sometimes in unexpected forms such as architecture and dance. Open your eyes to the symbolic language which surrounds us all, you will be surprised. As your mind opens up to a universal symbolic vocabulary you will find yourself discovering new depths in areas of human experience.

Your experience of the outer world will be reflected by the symbols which arise in the mind.

HELPLINE

I have found symbols from my meditation reappearing in my dream life. Is this usual?

This is a very common occurrence. It means that the symbols are being absorbed by consciousness even when you are not directly working on them.

I am not able to see pictures in my mind at all.

Everyone varies in their ability to visualise. People usually have a main system for representing experience which takes a visual, kinaesthetic, auditory and in some cases an olfactory form. Some people remember, evoke, dream and record their experiences as pictures. For others textures, sensations and physical responses have the power to evoke the imagination. Others recall the sounds of experiences, still others find that smell has the power to evoke both memory and imagination.

When we deliberately create an image in the mind either from memory or the imagination, we naturally combine these representational systems to build a picture to which we can respond.

The ability to visualise is the most common representational system. If it is not working for you, add kinaesthetic, auditory or even olfactory clues. In this way you will discover your main representational system which you can employ to create the inner symbolic landscapes.

Meditation in Judaism – The Qabalah

We have already seen how the Wheel of Life serves as a cosmogram, a symbolic depiction of both individual and cosmic forces, within Mahayana Buddhism. The Tree of Life, **Otz Chim** serves the same function within the mystical side of Judaism – **Qabalah**.

The Hebrew word **Qabalah** means both 'to receive' and 'to reveal'. Qabalah has been called the 'Yoga of the West'. It has also been described as a 'mighty, all-embracing glyph of the soul of Man and of the universe'. It is a complete metaphysical doctrine and philosophy presented in symbolic form. A modern Qabalist writes that 'its doctrines have spiritual contemplation, pure inspiration, or intellectual intuition as their point of departure and not the autocratic activity of reason'. In other words, the symbols of the Tree are brought to life within the meditative mind where they transcend reason and awaken the higher faculties.

The Tree of Life is composed of 10 spheres, called **sephira**, (**sephiroth** in the plural) with the addition of a hidden eleventh sphere. The sephiroth are interconnected by 22 pathways.

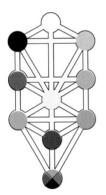

The Tree of Life.

The sephiroth bear archetypal names, The Crown, Wisdom, Understanding, Knowledge, Severity, Mercy, Beauty, Victory, Glory, Foundation, Kingdom. Complex symbols are assigned to each sephira and each path including numbers, colours, images, names and titles. Each sephira bears a different God-name representing a different aspect of deity. These too are used for meditation. For instance, the Kingdom is assigned the symbols of the four elements, the four colours olive, black, citrine and russet. Its Vice is avarice and inertia, its Virtue is discrimination. A young woman crowned and throned provides the so-called 'magical image' for this sephira. Its God-name is **Adonai ha Aretz** meaning Lord of Earth.

The student internalises these symbols through meditation and gradually absorbs those experiences related to each part of the tree. In so doing individual nature is transformed, the Microcosm and the Macrocosm are brought into alignment in accordance with the Hermetic maxim, 'As Above So Below'.

Western alchemical images represent spiritual processes through a symbolic code.

FINDING YOUR VOICE

'So let the Aum do its work and let all of you who can, employ it with frequency and with right thought so that the world purification may proceed apace.'

The Tibetan

Om yantra from Rajastan, 18th century.

The mantra

Now we will explore a different form of meditation – sound. Unlike the silent, introspective meditations we have tried up to now, this meditation is active and verbal.

The sounded meditation has a long and complex history. A single word or short phrase repeated over and over again as a focus for thought is called a **mantra**. There are both Eastern and Western mantras.

Om the Primal Sound; energy radiating from the ultimate bindu.

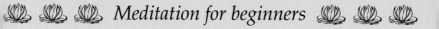

The Primal Om from Rajastan, 19th century.

The most famous mantra is probably **AUM** which was popularised in the West during the '60s. This short mantra holds a complete philosophy in itself, each letter being assigned to one of the major Hindu gods. The first letter A is assigned to **Brahman** the creator, the second letter U is assigned to **Vishnu**, the preserver, the third letter M is assigned to **Shiva**, the destroyer. The Aum mantra therefore represents the whole cycle of creation. It is regarded as the primal sound which generates all things.

43

This mantra is found in both Buddhism and Hinduism. It appears in another form in the well-known mantra, **Om Mane Padme Hum**, Hail to the Jewel in the Lotus. This refers to the jewel of enlightenment waiting to be unfolded from within the lotus of being. Mantras often have a profound meaning which is internalised as the mantra is sounded.

When a mantra is sounded it is vibrated. This is not singing. The sound is repeated slowly and deeply so that it resonates. The only way to learn this is by doing. When you try this you may find that the whole body seems to tingle after a while.

Sound is itself a vibration. Everything in the universe is itself vibrating. Nothing is still or quiescent. When we deliberately and consciously sound a mantra we are gradually changed by its dual aspect, meaning and vibration. As we internalise the concept represented by the mantra we absorb new ideas in consciousness. When we sound a mantra, we are in effect sounding a tuning fork within the subtle levels of our being. This establishes currents and waves within the energies of the body, and certain mantras, when correctly sounded, have the effect of changing our level of vibration.

18th century spiritual daggers used in rituals.

Human energies

We are in effect electromagnetic beings surrounded by an energy field which mirrors our total being. The electrical activity of the brain, heart and muscles contribute to this field. Valerie Hunt, a professor of kinesiology has worked extensively with human energies using electromyograms which measure the electrical muscular output. Normal biological activity produces muscle frequency at about 225 cycles per second and a heart frequency at about 250 cycles per second. Additionally she has recorded unexpected reading from individuals whose electrical energies were far beyond the norm. Twenty years of research has led her to correlate certain types of people with particular bands of electrical activity. She found that psychics and healers frequently fell within the band of 400–800 cycles per second. Interestingly trance mediums and chanellers fell within a very precise band, between rates of 800–900 cycles per second. Mystical personalities, who had a conscious sense of cosmic interconnectedness, manifested rates in excess of 900 cycles per second. By contrast, individuals with a mundane and distinct physical-based orientation produced slower frequencies up to about 250 cycles per second.

Research into the whole area of human energies is still in its infancy. Kirlian photography has proved to be a forerunner in this area. Individual researchers like Professor Hunt have done a great deal to establish evidence for the existence of the human energy field – the subtle life energies. These energies are responsive to concentrated thought and continuous interaction with other vibrations. Sound is vibration, mantra is sound. Mantra changes our vibration. A mantra does not function simply at an intellectual level. It is not a question of merely attempting to penetrate the meaning of the word. Sound itself is powerful.

The eighteenth century German pioneer Ernst Chladni was interested in the whole area of sound as vibration. He experimented by playing violin notes against metal discs covered with sand. He found that different notes produced different patterns. Clear, accurate notes produced clear patterns. Poorly sounded notes created only random and chaotic shifts in the sand. Significantly, the correct sounding of a mantra has always been important.

Hans Jenny, another pioneer in this area, developed a tonoscope which translated sounds into visual components. He found that the sound Aum when correctly vibrated produced a circular shape filled with a geometric pattern of circles and triangles, an extraordinary discovery when we look at the Sri Yantra, the traditional symbol for this mantra.

Directed sound is certainly powerful. It can destroy – soldiers must break step as they cross a bridge, a high note can shatter glass, a sound can start an avalanche. Other sounds have the power to heal and soothe. Music can alter the emotions. Music therapy is now well-established.

45

A Chladni disk – pattern created by sound.

A Sri Yantra.

Meditation bell from Tibet. The handle is decorated with vajra motifs. When the rim is rubbed the bell produces a continuous hum.

Exercise 11   Vibrating your name

Vibrate your own name out loud. Do it slowly. Repeat it several times. As you do this allow yourself to enter into your name. What do you learn by doing this? Do you like your name?

You may have found that vibrating your own name brought some realisations about yourself.

Spiritual traditions

Spiritual traditions often use the names of Gods as mantras in order to bring about a realisation into the nature of deity. In Sufism the sounded word is of central importance. The central practice is **Zikr**, the repetition of the Holy names. In the Qabalistic tradition, we also find several God-names which describe different aspects of deity. These God-names include **Eheieh** (pronounced Eh-hee-ee-yay), meaning 'I am that I am', **Shaddai el Chai**, meaning the 'Almighty Living God' and **Adonia ha Aretz**, meaning 'Lord of Earth'.

Every spiritual tradition has its own special sacred words and phrases. It is easy to forget that the West also has its own meditative tradition. The Christian Jesus prayer, 'Lord Jesus Christ, Son of God have Mercy on me a Sinner,' is a Western mantra. It originated with the Desert Fathers who were the earliest Christian hermits. The mantra is repeated over and over in time with the rhythm of the breath so that it is internalised into the heart of being. The Aramaic phrase, 'Maranatha' meaning, 'Come Lord' is another Christian mantra. It too can be synchronised with the breath.

A mantra is normally synchronised with the rhythm of the breath in order to create a natural pattern of sound and breath and to activate the subtle pranic energies of the body. **Prana**, the subtle aspect of the life force, can be directed through the controlled breath and the directed thought. Mantra encapsulates both; it employs the breath and the mind together. Meditation gradually increases sensitivity to pranic energies which are activated as an individual establishes the higher vibrational rates of being.

Exercise 12   Vibrating a mantra

Mantras have to be experienced, both as resonance and as meaning. Select a mantra for today and vibrate it deeply within yourself while dwelling upon its significance. You might be drawn to the Aum or Om mantra, the Christian Maranatha, or the Om Mane Padme Hum. Each mantra should be repeated while in the meditative state. Mantra meditation can be wonderful in a group when it is easy to become quite lost in the waves of sound.

Transcendental meditation

Transcendental Meditation (TM), by contrast, uses mantras which are specifically devoid of philosophical or religious meaning. Ideally the mantra is chosen and conferred by the guru. TM has many followers who claim that the daily repetition of the mantra has brought physical, emotional and spiritual benefit.

Chanting

We can of course use our voices in many ways, mantra being but one very specialised way. Chanting is a more general sounded meditation. In a group, chanting is both delightful and uplifting. Jill Purce, who has done a great deal to re-establish the tradition of sacred sound, says, 'To enchant means to make magical through chant. So by rediscovering our voices, we may both find our souls and re-enchant the world'.

The power of the voice

Finding your voice is part of the search for self. When you are confident that you always say what you mean and mean what you say, you are indeed true to yourself. However it is very easy to say only what is comfortable and socially acceptable.

We only need think of actors, singers and other professionals who direct the voice to realise its significance in communication. The voice, aside from the words we use, conveys our intentions and meaning at a subliminal level. Nervousness, self-confidence, fear, certainty, calmness, panic, authority, hesitation and many other states are all conveyed through subtle voice clues such as timbre, intonation, expression and delivery. Effective communication depends as much on the subtle clues encoded in the voice as the actual words that we use.

In Japan a person was traditionally judged to be unworthy and insincere unless the voice came from the hara centre, the belly. This centre represents a deep, instinctive level which transcends social veneer. Speaking from this level can only take place when we also breathe from the diaphragm and are in contact with the subtle life forces of this centre.

As we become more aware of the power of the voice, we should also become more conscious of what we actually say one to another. The Tibetan reminds us that, 'the purpose of speech is to clothe thought and thus make our thoughts available for others, speech reveals and right speech can create a form of beneficent purpose, just as wrong speech can produce a form which has a malignant objective.' Words have the power to wound through gossip, divide through half-truths, destroy through slander. The spoken word can uplift a nation, inspire a cause, change consciousness. As we seek to find our true voices, we should also attempt to discover the many purposes to which we may employ our own

---

HELPLINE

I am sounding a mantra but I can't seem to make it 'vibrate'.

Try to synchronise the sound with the breath. Use a deep full breath from the diaphragm. Imagine that the sound originates deep in the belly not the throat. Practise vibrating vowel sounds, these resonate quite easily. It is possible to purchase tapes of chanting. Hearing the real sound is a good way of learning what you are aiming for.

Meditation in Hinduism

The term Hindu simply means Indian. India is a vast country with many interwoven spiritual traditions including Buddhist and Jain influences. Hinduism does not have a founder or one single text, instead it is built upon a variety of inspirations. Its sacred texts include the **Upanishads**, which expound the nature of the God-head, the **Bhagavad-Gita**, which stresses man's duties in the world, the sagas of the **Ramayana** and the **Mahabharata**.

India is perhaps best known for its unique contribution to spiritual practice, Yoga and its attendant teachings, the **Sutras of Patanjali**, which established the Eight Limbs of Yoga. These are not unlike the requirements of the Noble Eightfold path of Buddhism. The steps outlined by both Patanjali and the Buddha placed meditation in a social and moral context.

The Eight Limbs of Yoga

Abstention – Yama
Observance – Niyama
Posture – Asana
Breath control – Pranayama
Sense withdrawal – Pratyahara
Concentration – Dharana
Meditation – Dhyana
Contemplation – Samadhi

There are several forms of yoga, **Jhana Yoga** being the path of the intellect, **Bhakti Yoga** the path of love and devotion, **Karma Yoga** the path of religious performance, **Hatha Yoga** the path of physical mastery, and **Raja Yoga** which controls the mind. Finally **Laya Yoga** activates the subtle energies. Each approach is considered to be equally valid, suited for different dispositions and types of people. India has such a wide variety of influences and spiritual avenues that it is almost impossible to point to just one path as being typical. There are Hindu monasteries and wandering solitary aesthetics, practitioners of yoga, devotees of particular deities and the classic fakirs and psychic showmen. Meditation plays a part to a lesser or greater degree in all aspects of Indian spiritual life.

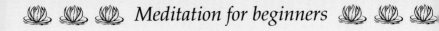

FINDING OTHERS

> 'Meditation is dangerous when the desire to serve is lacking.'
> *The Tibetan*

Avalokiteshvara, the Buddha of Compassion.

Service to others

In the Western tradition it is said that, 'We seek, to know in order to Serve'. This phrase itself is worth taking as a theme for meditation. We might like to think about the concept of service and how it applies to us.

The concept of service might be thought rather old-fashioned and dated today. The idea of 'doing your own thing' has become the slogan of a generation. Nevertheless the idea of putting others first is central to the great religions. In Mahayana Buddhism, the Bodhisattva willingly foregoes the state of nirvana, the ultimate goal, and returns into cyclic existence to help others. Christianity has always supported the weak, poor and sick. The Tibetan says, 'seek nothing for the separated self.'

If the concept of service appears outworn, we only have to imagine ourselves living in a society in which this ideal has faded. Values of self-aggrandisement, selfishness, survival, power and greed instead become the norm. Those too weak, too poor or too disadvantaged cannot compete in the human jungle. Who will serve them? If we seriously believe in the importance of self, we have become the victim of the ego. We absorb the values of the ego, separation, gratification and ego drive. We are caught in the vicious cycle of our own craving. The call of the Higher Self goes unheard. The demon Impermanence has us in his grip and is laughing at our folly.

It is too easy to forget that we each depend on other people, most often strangers, for even the smallest and most basic comforts in our life. Much of the food that we eat is grown in distant lands by people we do not know. Despite the fact that we will never meet the vast network of people who in reality help us, an invisible link nevertheless exists. In turn people whom we will never meet are also dependent upon our labour.

A Chinese character representing humanity is shown as two lines, one balanced upon the other. If one were to fall both would fall. What clearer image could there be of the interdependency of peoples? We can begin to discover others by simply reflecting upon the interdependency of peoples. Take the time to discover how many people are involved in your life in a single day. When we permit others to enter our consciousness we break the grip of the ego, if only momentarily.

The concept of service has perhaps never been more needed. Global communication keeps us in touch with the extended human family and its many trials throughout the world. We see the 'others' through media and news, often in tragic circumstances. If the term 'the human family', is ever to mean more than just an empty phrase, we have to realise that we are connected to all 'others'. It is often said that the coming Age of Aquarius will be characterised by a realisation of the human family. As each person makes this discovery for themselves so the Age of Aquarius will draw that much closer.

Exercise 13   Interdependency

You may find that even a simple exercise brings some far reaching realisations.

Enter into meditation. In your mind's eye recall the people who serve you in some way, no matter how small, in a single day. Try to remember everyone regardless of personal likes and dislikes. When you have done this discover those who depend on you even in a small way. Finally, imagine gossamer threads linking you all in a network of living dependency. You may be surprised to realise how far this network extends.

It is always easy to favour those whom we know and like. It is difficult to extend kindness to those who are strangers to us or those whom we may dislike. We have to work actively to overcome our feelings. Buddhism recognises that cherishing others is so unusual and difficult to achieve, that it can only be developed through mental training. An attitude of altruism based on love and compassion for all living things can only grow if we work to overcome those beliefs and blocks which serve as hindrances.

The biggest hindrance that we have to overcome as we learn to value others is our sense of separation which is clearly demonstrated through the physical senses. If we are truly separate there can be little value in developing altrusim, even less in just thinking about others whom we do not know. Our education and upbringing teaches us to look after ourselves first, to compete with others and to believe in ourselves. Such values have a use, but only within limits.

We have to make an effort to extend our thoughts towards those whom we do not know and will never meet. Buddhism suggests that we treat all sentient beings as if they had been good mothers to us – the thought is powerful, even startling. It provides a good starting point for the development of altruism.

All spiritual traditions emphasise the Opening of the Heart. It is considered to be the seat of compassion and transpersonal love. When the heart is closed, we are motivated by instinct, self-centred needs and personal drives. This produces goals and values that serve only the individual at the expense of the whole. When the heart is opened, we know that we are truly interdependent. When compassion, not separation, is the driving force, we experience a deep inner connection with Life itself. Altruism serves the whole in which we all share and benefit.

The global family.

Exercise 14   Friends and enemies

In order to break our value judgements, a Buddhist meditation asks us to examine what we really mean by the terms 'friend' and 'enemy'.

Imagine yourself in front of three people, an enemy, a friend and a neutral person. Evaluate your feelings towards each of them. You will probably feel love, dislike and indifference. These feelings will motivate your actions towards each of the people. Now try to examine the categories into which you have placed these different people. Are these categories to be immutable forever? What experiences and circumstances have led us to categorise these people in this way? What lessons do we learn by relating to people who represent these categories for us? From the friend we may learn to share, from the enemy we may learn inner strength, courage and endurance. These are qualities which often require adverse circumstances in order to develop. We should regard the bestower of these opportunities with thanks.

Exercise 15   The global family

The following meditation shows us a way of expanding our consciousness to include others. Sit in a meditative state and allow yourself to focus on your own life. Now become aware of your immediate neighbours. It does not matter if you don't know their names. Let your consciousness expand to include the people in your immediate neighbourhood. Imagine yourself with a bird's eye view, flying over the rooftops. It does not matter if these people are strangers to you, nor do your likes and dislikes have any relevance.

Continue to expand your consciousness to extend over your town or city. Now humanity has become an amorphous sea of unknown faces and unknown lives. Yet you also know that each of these lives is expressed through individuals with emotions, thoughts, hopes, needs and aspirations.

Now extend your consciousness to take in your whole country. See a map of your country in your mind's eye. Here is humanity en masse, teeming lives by the million. You do not need to know these people individually to know that human needs change little over the generations despite changes in outer circumstances.

Let your mind expand to cover the globe of the world. Let it roam freely over continents and countries. What do you find? What images fill your mind's eye? The rich and the poor, the starving and the fed, the sick and the healthy, the young and the old. This is humanity. Here are the others of our world.

Allow yourself to return to normal consciousness. Record your impressions and feelings.

Compassion

This meditation will surely have made you more aware of others and of
humanity as a whole. You probably will feel moved to offer help in some
way, yet also unable to help in a way sufficient to relieve the misery
which you have glimpsed. It is also very easy to forget others whom we
will of course never meet. However through meditation we can change
our inner awareness of others so that we can no longer forget. We can
generate those feelings that serve humanity within ourselves. In
meditation call to mind the misery and unhappiness of the human
condition. What positive qualities of the human heart can bring comfort?
If you were able to be present in dire human circumstances, what
positive feelings would such need evoke in you?

*Colossal seated buddha in meditation posture from Kamakura,
Japan, 13th century. The Buddha taught the importance of
compassion for all living things.*

Who could fail to experience the loving kindness of the open heart. It is the same feeling with which we hold a newborn child. This quality of loving kindness is the basis for compassion – universal loving-kindness. Extend this feeling within yourself as far as you are able to those in need.

Compassion will only take root when we allow it to do so. The development of emotional qualities through meditation is no fanciful escapism. We are in fact changing ourselves. We are more prepared to meet need in others when we meet it face to face; we have more understanding of the human condition. By generating compassion in ourselves we in fact generate compassion to the world.

Compassion and loving kindness begin in small ways, like the tiny seed of a great tree. Simply ask yourself, 'Who may I help today?' You have tended the seed of service within yourself.

Should you ever doubt the value of compassion, simply imagine yourself as being poor and weak in a society that values only survival, competition and strength.

HELPLINE

Are there any pitfalls to look out for?
Practice should not permit you to feel 'special'. Feelings of righteous self-congratulation will destroy the worth of your practice. Feeling 'better' than people who do not share your path is a sign of ego inflation. Nor do you have to advertise what you do by decking yourself with symbols. There is a saying in Buddhism, 'transform your inner viewpoint, but leave your external appearance as it is'.

Meditation in Christianity

Many Christians seem to feel dubious about meditation. It is not generally found in ordinary Sunday worship which consists of prayers, singing and a sermon. This is a pity as Christianity has a fine and long history of meditative practice and spiritual exercises. It has also produced a number of noted mystics. Christianity offers many deep philosophical concepts such as the Love of God, Redemption and the Sonship of Christ. Without reflective thought, these will remain empty phrases, pure dogma devoid of substance.

Christian meditation originated with the Desert Fathers, the early Christian hermits who established the basis for the Christian withdrawn life. The Jesus Prayer, a Western mantra, originated with the Desert

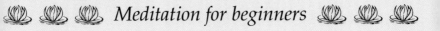

Christ on the Cross, Albrecht Durer (1471–1528).

Fathers. It is repeated and internalised as it is synchronised with the breath. In common with the Aum mantra, it too expresses a philosophy; it enshrines the heart of Christian belief. The Jesus prayer is centred at the heart but suffuses through the whole being. St Simeon recommends the following procedure:

> 'Sit down alone and in silence. Lower your head, shut your eyes, breathe out gently and imagine yourself looking into your own heart. Carry your mind from your head to your heart. As you breathe out say "Lord Jesus Christ, have mercy on me." Say it moving your lips, or simply say it in your mind. Be calm, patient and repeat the process very frequently.'

Christianity is not without its sacred images either. In the Eastern Orthodox tradition, the icon is still used as a focus for meditation and devotion. Icon painting is a sacred tradition which embodies the highest Christian principles.

Ignatius Loyola, founder of the Jesuits, devised a series of spiritual exercises designed to be used over a four-week period in retreat. Loyola applied the principle of the creative imagination to the life of Christ so that in meditation the individual might respond in a personal way to the scenes from the life of Christ. For example, the instructions for the meditation on the birth of Christ begin as follows, 'Represent to yourself in imagination the road from Bethlehem, in length and breadth. Is it level or through valleys or over hillsides? In the same way study the place of the Nativity. Is the cave spacious or cramped, low or high?'

The series of meditations continues from the Nativity to the familiar scenes of the Passion, Crucifixion and Resurrection. The principle is exactly the same as that used to create inner landscapes in the mind's eye.

FINDING THE WORLD

'The world situation is such, the problems and uncertainty are such that scarcely a person in the world at this time is exempt.
Everyone is more or less involved in the planetary situation.'

The Tibetan

Global consciousness

Meditation may appear to be a solitary pursuit even when it is performed in groups. However, far from being an isolating or self-centred activity, meditation brings expansion and connection to others. Meditation inescapably brings the world into your heart. Meditators have always known this.

We live upon one world and breathe one air, yet we consciously divide all that we have into 'mine' and 'not mine'. We are convinced by the illusion of separation. We are steadfastly wedded to territorial principles. Global consciousness, on the other hand, unites where we choose to divide, connects where we choose to isolate and unifies where we choose to fragment.

Mystics through the ages have recorded the personal experience of unity and affirmed the wholeness of all creation. Such individuals were not informed by global communication or holistic philosophy. Yet testaments of mystical experience from all traditions and times tell us what we have only recently come to know, that Life is a Unity which takes on the appearance of a myriad of forms.

Recently, a representative for the American space programme remarked that one of the most unexpected results of ventures into space had been the tangible sense of awe experienced by the astronauts who looked upon the world turning in space. It was for them a moment of genuine **satori**, the eruption of a new perspective in the classical and time-honoured tradition. This image has the power to do the same for anyone who sees it through the eyes of meditation.

The first view of the world from space marked a breakthrough for human consciousness. The image is indelibly marked in the minds of all those who have seen it. For children growing up alongside this image, the world suspended in space is as common as nursery rhymes or a cartoon character. Star Trek and other science fiction bring the notion of global consciousness right into the living room. If we are not careful, we may even lose the real impact of the image. Familiarity always breeds contempt. We begin to take the miraculous for granted.

The Earth – our home.

Exercise 16   Planet Earth

Sit before the image of the world until it is clear in your mind. Close your eyes, hold the image in your mind. Now allow your thoughts to dwell upon the image before you. There is much to discover. Record your thoughts and feelings at the end of the meditation. Meditating upon the world in this way is so rich a source for inspiration that you can return to it many times. You may also experience very deep emotions like the astronauts themselves.

From this perspective of course the world appears as a whole, a unity. As we descend from this exalted perspective we tend to lose this sense of oneness. Daily life too often brings a sense of separation. Life appears to be fragmented and we lose our sense of participation in the whole. Meditation re-establishes an internal sense of belonging. Consciousness knows no physical boundaries. Mystical consciousness is characterised by a sense of unity.

When we begin to search for the world, we should remind ourselves of the one question that has taunted philosophers and physicists alike. What is matter made of? The extraordinary scientific knowledge available today provides a fascinating insight into the enigma of matter. It cannot be divided into ever smaller parts, for there comes a point where we break though the sub-atomic threshold to a confusing world where things are not always what they seem. It is this sea of energy which gives birth to matter. The sub-atomic world is our own world. It bears more than a passing likeness to the Void, Shunyata the ultimate realisation of Buddhism. Whenever we contemplate the world around us, we might remember that according to Hindu philosophy we are contemplating Maya, the world of illusion, the plane of effect not cause. Whenever we become swept up by the physicality of matter, and carried away by the conviction of permanence, we should remember that all is in a state of constant motion, continuous activity, total movement. Permanence is the illusion.

The world outside begins at the front door. We have the opportunity to experience the physical world which too often goes without notice. We can meditate in the park, in the garden, by the sea, by a river, on a walk. When we really hear the birds sing, observe the leaves open, watch the blossom burst, step into new snow, we truly enter into the quality of the moment.

Life is not confined to the human family. The animal, vegetable and even mineral kingdoms partake of life. We can become aware of lives other than our own by opening the eye of perception to the rich manifestations of life which are everywhere.

Meditation upon the extraordinary events and processes of the natural world creates a living relationship between the individual and the physical world. There can be no doubt that we as a species have endangered our own future existence though thoughtless plunder, greedy consumption and the total disregard for natural balance and harmony. It is only through discovering our own respect and awe for Nature that we may come to realise the results of our choices and actions. When we start paying homage we will stop destroying.

Exercise 17   Experiencing nature

When outside, open your mind to everything that is around you. You may discover grass, shrubs or trees each teeming with minute life. The ground beneath your feet is home to subterranean life. Perhaps you will hear birds and insects or see small animals, each living out their existence. Perhaps you will see flowers, all following a different life cycle. Become aware of all that surrounds you. Become aware of the delicate balance and interconnectedness between all the life forms around you. Record your thoughts and realisations. What feelings did you experience as you attempted to expand your consciousness in this way?

Everything has its own lifecycle from a microbe to a star. In your imagination you can recreate the experience of any life form, animate or otherwise. Children do this quite spontaneously. Unfortunately, adults have usually long forgotten how to be a dolphin, dodo or dinosaur.

Our experience is always limited by physical constraints. Consciousness, however, is never limited except by self-imposed limitations. We cannot meet all humanity but we can develop our relationship to humanity through meditation. We cannot experience all the faces of nature but we can foster our feelings for the natural world through meditation.

Buddhism actively generates the quality of compassion for all sentient beings in many ways. In the **Metta Sutta**, the discourse on loving-kindness, the qualities of loving kindness, compassion, joy and equanimity are first generated and then radiated outwards to the six directions. This type of meditation can be experienced in the following way. It is not a cold intellectual practice but a warm, heart-centred affirmation of shared being.

Exercise 18   Radiating love

Sit quietly and first generate a feeling of loving kindness within yourself. Turn your attention outwards from yourself to others. Radiate the feeling that you have generated. Imagine a wave of living light radiating from the level of the heart. Now feel light radiating out before you into infinity in an unbroken wave. Generate the same loving energy in waves of light from behind, from your left, from your right, above you and below you. Imagine that these waves of living energy pass into infinity, bringing the touch of human warmth wherever they pass. Record your experience.

Who can fail to be aware of the difficulties of the world as a whole today – famine, pollution, poverty, environmental problems seem overwhelming at times. Too often as individuals we feel helpless in the face of such monumental issues. It is true that perhaps we are physically limited. Yet consciousness is never limited. Ideas must precede action, energy follows thought.

The illusion of separation exerts a powerful grip. We feel isolated. All efforts seem wasted and futile. To counteract the negative and depressing impact of this, we can instead think of ourselves as individual cells in a great body. We each have a role to play in the well-being of the whole.

Meditation helps us to find out who are. When we know that we are free to be ourselves. In actively being ourselves we can fulfil our role both for ourselves and for the whole, 'As Above so Below'. The notion of separation is as illusory as a mirage. One of the most powerful, hopeful and indeed extraordinary concepts of recent times is that of the Planetary Network of Light, the New World Servers. This idea permeates the teachings of the Tibetan. Members are physically unknown to each other, linked only by the power of their aspiration to serve the world, focused through regular loving meditation. 'How shall one qualify, first learn to practise harmlessness; then desire nothing for the separated self and thirdly look for the sign of divinity in all.' Your true aspiration can connect you.

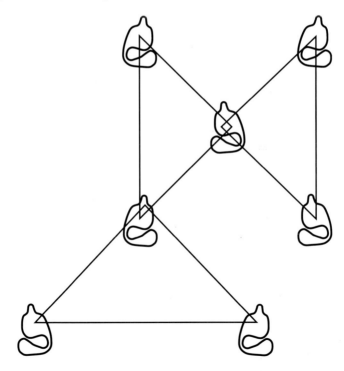

The Planetary Network of Light.

Exercise 19   The planetary network

Only do this meditation if you feel highly motivated by a genuine compassion and desire to serve. Performed regularly over a period of time, this meditation brings a sense of connection and genuine contact with other minds. Do not think that envisaging the network is mere escapism from the problems of the world – it might just prove to be your first step towards helping to solve some of them.

Enter a meditative state. The Planetary Network can be visualised as a gossamer web of white light in exactly the same form as in the earlier exercise. Allow this network to extend over the whole globe. See yourself as a nodal point in the web. Pour your own love commitment into the web of light. Imagine other people around the world doing exactly the same thing. Record your experience.

Earth, air, fire and water

We will continue to think about our place in the world. You may return to this theme over and over again. You can approach this relationship in many ways. Ideally go out and be with nature. You can also discover more about the world by meditating on the four elements of earth, air, fire and water. This fourfold representation is found in both Eastern and Western traditions. In the Eastern tradition, the elements are represented by the tattvas which are symbolic images. The element of earth is represented by a yellow square, the element of air by a blue circle, the element of fire by a red triangle and the element of water by a silver crescent.

In the Western tradition, the element of earth is represented by a disc inscribed with a five pointed star, itself a symbol of humankind. The element of air is represented by a sword, that which incisively cuts. The element of water is symbolised by a cup and the element of fire by a rod or staff.

You can of course represent the elements in your own way. You may meditate on each of the elements in turn representing them if you wish by real objects which can be a focus for your thoughts. It would be natural to use a small bowl of water, a dish of earth, a lighted candle and a stick of incense to represent the elements. You can also meditate on the unity of the four elements by drawing a circle with the names of the elements on the edge. In a meditative state allow your mind to focus on these four as aspects of the one. You can repeat this many times, there is so much to discover. Write down all your thoughts when the meditation is over. When you have meditated upon each of the four elements in turn and also as a synthesis, you can include a fifth element. In the Eastern tradition this is called **Akasa**, spirit. In the Western tradition it is called **Ether** or consciousness, sometimes symbolised by the Holy Grail. The relationship between matter and consciousness is the very enigma of creation. The world awaits you.

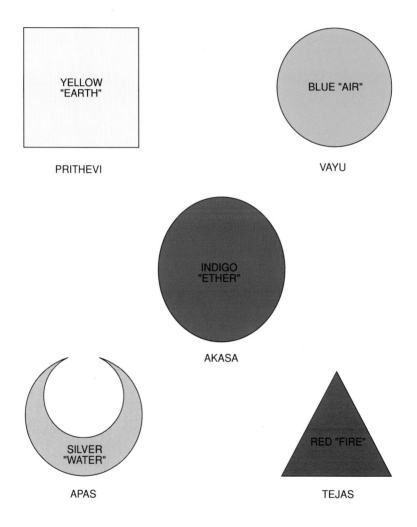

The Eastern Tattvas.

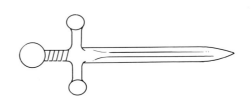

The Western Elemental Symbols.

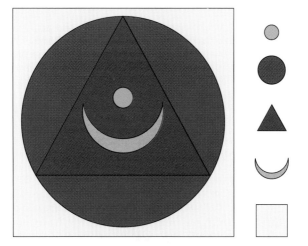

The elements in combination including the symbol for akasa, spirit or ether.

HELPLINE

Since I have started meditation I have developed what are usually termed psychic faculties. Is this something to worry about?
As consciousness expands, we are able to function at higher levels of vibration. Psychic faculties are regarded as diversions on the path towards enlightenment. They should be accepted but not sought, integrated but not indulged. These gifts may also be used in the service of others, particularly if the ability to heal is awakened.

Meditation in Islam

Islam has its own mystical path which incorporates spiritual exercises and practices including meditation. This is the way of **Sufism**. The Sufi way is rooted in the Qur'an (Koran) and the teachings of the prophet. At its heart, Sufism expresses the Unity of Being, whole and indivisible, 'there is no God but God'. Sufism has been eclectic in its influences, absorbing other mystical traditions. Pythagoran teachings, Hermetic writings and Zoroastrian influences have each been absorbed into the Sufi way.

The Sufi path has three main elements, doctrine, initiation and method. Sufi doctrine is based on the Qur'an but also includes commentaries made upon it by individual masters. The teacher–pupil relationship remains central. It is the only recognised path to initiation. The master alone has the right to initiate as he stands in the place of the prophet at the rite of rebirth into the spiritual life. The power to initiate is derived from Muhammad through a chain of transmission which, like apostolic succession, stretches back in time. It is considered to be the guarantee of authenticity.

It is impossible to extract typically Sufi meditations from Sufi philosophy. Meditation techniques vary widely. The individual master has the authority to choose suitable methods for different students. The aim of meditation, **fikr**, is to prevent the mind from going astray while the heart concentrates on God. The main practice is **zikr**, the active invocation of the presence of God through the repetition of the Holy Names. Zikr means to mention, to invoke and to remember. The spoken word is very important as a vehicle for realisation. The Sufi tradition is rich with poem, symbolic tale and allegory.

The study of symbols

Great value is attached to the study of symbols. It is perhaps the most important Sufi science. The journey of the soul is symbolically described in The Gardens of Paradise which encompass the Garden of the Soul, the Garden of the Heart, the Garden of the Spirit and the Garden of the Essence. In the Paradisal Gardens, the soul encounters The Tree of Immortality, the Fountain of Knowledge and other symbolic representations.

Everyday activities also become symbolic containers for meditation. Poetry, calligraphy, rug weaving, dance, even geometry and architecture reveal sacred truths and universal principles which speak volumes to the awakened mind and heart. In this tradition, all is sacred, unity is everywhere expressed.

FINDING A NEW DIRECTION

'May light and love and power shine upon your ways.'

The Tibetan

You have now completed a course of meditation practice and have tried several approaches – the non-focused zazen, the structured guided visualisation, the sounded meditation, and others. Now is the time to gather up what you have learned through these varied experiences and look to the future. What have you learned about yourself? What have you learned about your mind? In the short time you have been able to give to meditation so far, you will probably have experienced boredom, frustration and confusion. You may also have sensed new possibilities, touched a moment of complete peace, experienced life more keenly and fully.

You might want to find out more about meditation. There are plenty of good books on the subject now. Meditation cannot be learned quickly. In fact there is nothing that can really be mastered in a short space of time. It is possible only to uncover a genuine interest and make a decision to continue with it. Teachers and groups exist. The new student is not alone – there are many possibilities for the genuine student.

Time

In this final chapter we will focus on the quality of time. In Eastern traditions, time is often depicted in monstrous form. Our lives are slowly devoured by this monster. In many ways our lives are ruled by external time. We are a society of obsessive clock watchers, an unavoidable condition for people who simply have to be on time all the time. The clock, the timetable and the crammed diary make good servants but bad masters. Our life is marked by time – birthdays and Christmas celebrations pace the year out. One year follows another and before we know it, we feel that time is no longer on our side. Time, of course need not be the relentless enemy but the bestower of opportunity. It all depends on our perspective. Meditation can bring a new perspective into our lives.

The Monster of Time.

Exercise 20   *The seed of the future*

This meditation will bring you a sense of your future direction. Enter into a meditative state. Be aware of your surroundings, even though your eyes may be closed. Be aware of any sounds reaching you, perhaps the sounds of traffic, bird song, distant voices. Become aware of yourself in time and space. Now imagine your consciousness expanding through the limitations of the room to the world beyond. Here other lives are to be found, human, animal, vegetable and even mineral. You share this moment with all life everywhere. Let your consciousness continue to move outwards beyond any physical confines. This moment teems with life. Life is everywhere. You are part of this great current. You have a part to play in the unfolding future. The future grows out of the present moment. **Your** future may grow out of this moment. Allow yourself a few moments to dwell upon your own deep aspirations. Let your deepest

Mahakala, the Power of Devouring Time, Tibet, 18th century.

thoughts surface. Where does your deepest commitment lie? What will you truly seek to do with the time given into your hands? Through time you can become the person you were always intended to be. This moment contains as many possibilities as you permit. Record your deepest thoughts.

Time slips through our fingers so easily unless we make a conscious relationship with the passing of time. Seasonal markers can be far more than mere festivity. We have the opportunity to review the passing of our time and the passage of life. Seasonal markers give us a sense of place and direction. The cosmic clock gives us a sense of annual rhythm. The four landmarks of the year, spring and autumn equinox, summer and winter solstice, provide natural times for reflection and meditation. At the vernal equinox we can meditate upon rebirth and renewal. At midsummer we can reflect upon activity and fruition. In the autumn we

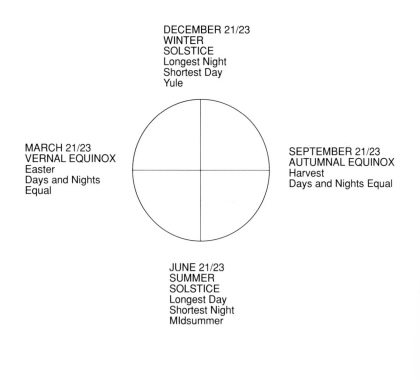

DECEMBER 21/23
WINTER
SOLSTICE
Longest Night
Shortest Day
Yule

MARCH 21/23
VERNAL EQUINOX
Easter
Days and Nights
Equal

SEPTEMBER 21/23
AUTUMNAL EQUINOX
Harvest
Days and Nights Equal

JUNE 21/23
SUMMER
SOLSTICE
Longest Day
Shortest Night
MIdsummer

The Cosmic Clock.

can reflect upon the personal harvest. At midwinter we can meditate upon the value of latency and the imminent appearance of light from the depths of darkness.

This fourfold pattern can become a primary foundation for aligning ourselves to the natural cycle of the year. The passing of time becomes meaningful when it is welcomed and celebrated. However, ultimately it is our being in the here and now which enables us to make the most of each day.

In the Western Mystery Tradition it is common practice to review each day as it has passed. This exercise performed at the end of each day develops detachment, self-awareness and a sense of the value of time.

Exercise 21   Reviewing the day

At the end of the day enter into a meditative state of mind. Play back the events of the day in your mind's eye. It will be only natural to comment on your own actions during the day. See yourself as objectively as possible. Finally evaluate not what you took out of the day but what you put into it.

Meditation – the ultimate goal

Meditation has much to offer any individual. The physical, emotional and psychological benefits that come from regular meditation bring changes which help us to cope with our busy lives. The calm state in which meditation takes place is itself beneficial to mind and body. It can be likened to a sanctuary. This is not the rest of sleep but the peace of stillness under conscious control. We all seek peace, especially in the face of difficult circumstances. Artificial calmness can be prescribed for us. It is illusory.

Body awareness will develop as we create a more conscious relationship with ourselves. Too often we are only aware of the body when things begin to go wrong. Instead we can use the meditative state to affirm well-being. Meditation also vivifies the subtle energies which underpin the physical foundation. Energy follows thought.

Stress is built into our lives. Employment, unemployment, financial responsibilities, relationships, prospects and expectations can all bring feelings of anxiety and crisis. We have to develop coping mechanisms or the roller coaster of circumstances will carry us into ill health and depression. Meditation brings a sense of reality and proportion into life, our best defence against the values of society which stresses competition, acquisition and materialism. When we come to understand who we are and what we value, we can look objectively upon the values of society as presented by education, parents, media and even peers.

The Bo tree beneath which Buddha was enlightened.

Adolescence is the time to create the foundation for a value system. This age group is increasingly targeted as a consumer market and encouraged to develop materialistic needs. Those who are not able to join in are excluded and become easy prey for the many traps which lie in wait.

It is worth reminding ourselves that meditation grew from societies which were and still are very poor in a material sense. In these societies meditation transcends conditions of poverty. We have to transcend our wealth which is possibly a harder task. True values are neither dependent on poverty nor wealth; both are illusory.

The ultimate goal of meditation is an awakening into the state of enlightenment. Buddha himself attained enlightenment as he sat beneath the Bo tree. Buddhism grew directly from the meditation of Siddhartha Gautama, so it is not surprising that Buddhism lays so much stress on the practice of meditation.

Enlightenment means very little for most of us. It is often symbolised by a lotus flower. The lotus is a beautiful flower rather like a water-lily. We can draw upon this symbol in our last meditation. The lotus will give us an image of our own growth, direction, spiritual aspiration and imminent divine beauty.

The lotus is a wonderful representation of the spiritual journey. It shows us that the journey which takes place in time and space also takes place within personal consciousness. A thousand petalled lotus is often depicted at the top of the head. This represents our ultimate nature, each petal representing a quality of being. This lotus is called the Crown. When fully opened it represents our crowning achievement. Even when we are unaware of its presence, it represents our potentiality. We are reminded of the journey still to come and the possibilities within the future.

Meditation will, in time, bring about a total transformation of being. You can unfold the many qualities that are hidden within and become the person you were always intended to be.

The lotus is a symbol of enlightenment.

Exercise 22   The lotus of enlightenment

Allow yourself to enter a meditative state. Imagine that you sit beside a shallow lotus pool. The surface of the pool is dotted with lotus plants. Most are closed, tightly budded upon the surface. A few are beginning to open, revealing a glimpse of creamy white beauty. One lotus catches your eye. It is in full bloom; its many petals lay open to the sunlight. It is quite beautiful.

You allow your eye to descend into the waters beneath the surface. The waters are shallow and you see that these wonderful plants are all rooted in the mud. Each plant must make its way to the surface. Only then can it flower, revealing its true beauty. Sustained in the darkness, nourished by the depths, the lotus root will generate a humble shoot which will rise to the heights to reveal its natural beauty. Here is the symbol of the enlightened mind reaching up for light, awakening from the depths, fulfilling its own nature. Record your own thoughts.

When we are out in the world, we should not forget to bring the meditational state of mind to bear. Full concentration, full awareness and total mindfulness enrich all life activities whether at work or in leisure time. Meditation is not a withdrawal from life, but a way of deepening our experience of life.

HELPLINE

Do I have to give up the things of the world to aspire towards enlightenment?
You do not have to give up the things of the world, only your attachment to them. In other words you may possess your possessions but do not let them possess you. Enlightenment takes place in the world where it is most needed, although there may be times when it can be helpful to retreat in order to strengthen the meditative life.

The universal principles of meditation

Despite the fact that meditation takes many forms which can appear to be contradictory at times, there are universal principles which are to be found in all systems.

The whole being is actively applied in meditation, not merely the rational mind. Posture and breathing are brought into consciousness and incorporated into practice. The mind is used actively to explore, dwell upon and be absorbed by a wide variety of focus points. These serve to develop concentration, sharpen insight, break illusions and begin the process of transformation at all levels of being which culminates in the birth of the true being.

Meditation can only be learned through experience. Words are no more than signposts. I wish you well as you set out on the most valuable journey of all, to find out who you are.

Statue of Buddha with a lotus emblem.

SUGGESTED READING

Chapter 1
A Western Approach to Zen,
Christmas Humphreys: Unwin
Mandala 1985
How to Meditate, Lawrence
LeShan; Crucible Books 1989

Chapter 2
Mahayana Buddhism, Beatrice
Lane Suzuki; Unwin Mandala 1990
Introducing Buddhism, Chris
Pauling; Windhorse 1990

Chapter 3
Creating Mandalas, S. Fincher;
Shambhala Pubns 1992
The Living Qabalah, Will Parfitt;
Element 1988

Chapter 4
Hinduism, K M Sen; Penguin Books
1991
*The Essential Teachings of
Hinduism*, Kerry Brown; Arrow
Books 1990

Chapter 5
Christian Mysticism, William
McNamara; Element 1991
Mysticism East and West, Rudolf
Otto; Quest 1987

Chapter 6
The Sufi Way to Self-Unfoldment,
S F Haeri; Element 1987
*Sufism – The Mystical Doctrines
and Methods of Islam*, W Stoddart;
Aquarian 1976

Chapter 7
*Cutting Through Spiritual
Materialism*, Chogym Trungpa;
Shambala 1987
The Meditators Handbook, Dr D
Fontana; Element 1992
Return to the Centre, Bede
Griffiths; Collins 1984

ORGANISATIONS

Sivananda Yoga Vedanta Centre
51 Foulsham Road
Putney
LONDON
SW15 1AZ
Tel: 0181-780 0160

Sri Chinmoy Centre
Run and Become
42 Palmer Street
LONDON
SW1 0AB
Tel: 0181-876 6049
There are also centres in Oxford,
Cambridge, Bristol, Ipswich,
Edinburgh and Birmingham. The
Sri Chinmoy Centre organises
workshops, concerts and races.

The Buddhist Society
publishes The Buddhist Directory
listing Buddhist and Zen centres in
the UK and Ireland at £5 inc p&p.
58 Eccleston Square
LONDON
SW1V 1PH
Tel: 0171-834 5858

A list of international groups is
held on database by
Wisdom Books
402 Hoe Street
LONDON
E17 9AA
Tel: 0181-520 5588

Transcendental Meditation
TM Freepost
LONDON
SW1P 4YY
Tel: Freephone 0800 269303

The Arcane School
founded in 1923 by Alice Bailey. Its
work is based on the received
works of the Tibetan.
Suite 54
3 Whitehall Court
LONDON
SW1A 2EF

The Samatha Association
c/o 29 Chandos Road
Chorlton-cum-Hardy
MANCHESTER
M21 1SS
Tel: 0161-881 0038
Samatha meditation is based on
developing attention to the breath.
Local classes are held in Bolton,
Cambridge, Chester, Durham,
London, Liverpool, Manchester,
Oxford, Rossendale, Stockport.

Christian Meditation Centre
29 Campden Hill Road
LONDON
W8 7DK
Tel: 0171-937 0014

The Julian Meetings
Send sae for full address list to:
Hilary Wakeman
32 Grosvenor Road
Norwich
NORFOLK
NR2 2PZ

Sufism
London Sufi Centre for Holistic
Arts and Sciences
21 Lancaster Road
LONDON
W11 1QL
Tel: 0171-221 3215

The Community Health Foundation
188 Old Street
LONDON
EC1V 9BP
Tel: 0171-251 4076

Samye Ling
This is the first Tibetan Buddhist
Centre and temple in the Western
world.
Eskerdale Muir
Langholm
DUMFRIESSHIRE
Scotland
DG13 0QL

ORGANISATIONS

Greater Washington, DC Assoc. of
Professionals Practising the
Transcendental Meditation
Program
4818 Montgomery Lane
Bethesda, MD 20814

S. Boncheff, Chmn.
Tel: 202-785-5144

American Buddhist Assoc.
1151 W. Leland Ave.
Chicago, IL. 60640

Rev. Sunnan Kubose
Tel: 312-334-4661

American Buddhist Movement
301 W 45th St.
New York, NY 10036

Dr. Kevin R. O'Neil-Pres.
Tel: 212-489-1075

Buddhist Churches of America
Federation of Buddhist Women's
Assoc.
c/o Buddhist Churches of America
1710 Octavia St.
San Francisco, CA 94109

Rev. Soikan Fukuma Exec. Dir.
Tel: 415-776-5600

First Zen Institute of America
113 E. 30th St.
New York, NY 10016

Mary Farkas
Tel: 212-686-2520

**Friends of the Western Buddhist
Order**
c/o Aryaloka Retreat Center
Heartwood Cir.
Newmarket, NH. 0387

Dh. Manjuvajra, Chm.
Tel: 603-659-5456

GLOSSARY

Brahma   Hindu God, the Creator.
Buddha   A title meaning awakened or enlightened one.

Dorje   Tibetan sceptre, the 'noble stone'.

Fikr   The Sufi term for meditation.

Hinayana   A school of Buddhism meaning the lesser vehicle.

Mahayana   A school of Buddhism meaning the greater vehicle.
Mandala   A Sanskrit term meaning circle, a circular image depicting universal forces used in meditation.
Mantra   A sacred word or phrase used as a meditation.
Maranatha   Aramaic phrase meaning 'Come Lord'.
Menorah   The seven-branched candlestick of Judaic tradition.
Metta sutta   The discourse of loving kindness.

Qabalah   The mystical teachings of Judaic tradition.

Satipatthana   'Mindfulness' or 'awareness'.
Shi-ne   A Tibetan meditation technique.
Shiva   Hindu god, the Destroyer.
Satori   An awakening to the state of enlightenment.

Tattvas   The subtle elements of the universe.
The Tibetan   The guiding mind behind the received works of Alice Bailey.
Theravada   The major Hinayana School of Buddhism meaning Teaching of the Elders.

Vajra   The thunderbolt or diamond.
Vajravana   A school of Buddhism meaning the diamond vehicle.
Vishnu   Hindu God, the Preserver.
Vantra   A geometric diagram expressing cosmic principles used in meditation.

Zazen   'Just sitting', a foundation practice in Zen Buddhism.
Zikr or **Dhikr**   The practice of remembrance of God through the invocation of divine names.